Super SHEROES OF SCIENCE

Exploring Space

Women Who Led the Way

NANCY DICKMANN

Children's Press®
An imprint of Scholastic Inc.

Library of Congress Cataloging-in-Publication Data
Names: Dickmann, Nancy, author.
Title: Exploring space : women who led the way / Nancy Dickmann.
Description: First edition. | New York, NY : Children's Press, an imprint of Scholastic Inc., 2022. |
   Series: Super SHEroes of science | Includes bibliographical references and index. | Audience: Ages 8-10. |
   Audience: Grades 4-6. | Summary: Audience: Ages 8-10. | Audience: Grades 4-6. | Summary: "This brand-new
   series highlights some of the major contributions women have made in the world of science. Photographs
   throughout"— Provided by publisher.
Identifiers: LCCN 2021037467 (print) | LCCN 2021037468 (ebook) | ISBN 9781338800319 (library binding)
   | ISBN 9781338800326 (paperback) | ISBN 9781338800333 (ebk)
Subjects: LCSH: Women astronauts—Biography—Juvenile literature. | Women scientists—Biography—
   Juvenile literature. | Women in astronautics—History—Juvenile literature. |
   BISAC: JUVENILE NONFICTION / Biography & Autobiography / Women
Classification: LCC TL793 .D493 2022 (print) | LCC TL793 (ebook) | DDC
   629.450092/2—dc23
LC record available at https://lccn.loc.gov/2021037467
LC ebook record available at https://lccn.loc.gov/2021037468

Picture credits:
Photos ©: cover top: Sahar Coston-Hardy; cover center top: James Estrin/The New York Times/Redux; cover center bottom: Colorization
by Robin Clark; cover bottom: Colport/Alamy Images; 5 left: Sahar Coston-Hardy; 5 center left: James Estrin/The New York Times/
Redux; 5 center right: Colorization by Robin Clark; 5 right: Colport/Alamy Images; 6 inset top: Colorization by Robin Clark; 6 bottom:
Sarin Images/The Granger Collection; 7 top: SZ Photo/Scherl/Bridgeman Images; 8 center: The Granger Collection; 9 top: US Patent and
Trademark Office; 10 bottom: Smith Collection/Gado/Getty Images; 11 top: Bettmann/Getty Images; 12 top left: Colorization by Robin
Clark; 14 inset top: Colport/Alamy Images; 15 right: The Print Collector/Getty Images; 16 top: USPTO/Wikimedia; 19 top: E.D. Torial/
Alamy Images; 20 inset top: USPTO/Wikimedia; 21 top: Scott McPartland/Getty Images; 22 top: US Patent and Trademark Office; 24 top:
Harold M. Lambert/Getty Images; 26 inset top: James Estrin/The New York Times/Redux; 27 bottom: Adam Glanzman/Bloomberg/Getty
Images; 28 bottom: Bettmann/Getty Images; 31 top: Drew Angerer/Getty Images; 32 top: World Economic Forum/Sikarin Thanachaiary/
Flickr; 34 top: Library of Congress; 34 bottom: Marion O'Brien Donovan Papers/Archives Center/National Museum of American History/
Smithsonian Institution; 35 top: Science Source; 35 bottom: Dan Goshtigian/The Boston Globe/Getty Images; 36 top: Hagley Archive/
Science Source; 37 top: Sahar Coston-Hardy; 37 bottom: Bettina Strenske/Alamy Images; 38 top: Courtesy of Azza Abdel Hamid Faiad; 39
top: Matt Nager/Redux; 40 top left: INTERFOTO/Alamy Images; 41 top right: Kevin Dietsch/UPI/Alamy Images; 41 bottom right: Kathryn
Scott/The Denver Post/Getty Images; 42-43: pop_jop/Getty Images; 44 top left: Colorization by Robin Clark; 44 center: James Estrin/
The New York Times/Redux; 45 top: Sahar Coston-Hardy.

All other photos © Shutterstock.

10 9 8 7 6 5 4 3 2 1   22 23 24 25 26

Printed in the U.S.A. 113
First edition, 2022
Series produced for Scholastic by Parcel Yard Press

Contents

Super SHEroes Change the World

Women scientists, **engineers**, and inventors have made remarkable breakthroughs for centuries. Often, however, their achievements went unrecognized. Today far more women work in these fields than ever before, and their achievements are celebrated.

This book celebrates the life and the work of twelve of these women, twelve Super SHEroes of Science! They all worked, or still work, to explore space.

Space is everything found beyond Earth's atmosphere. It is also called outer space, and it includes stars, moons, galaxies, black holes, and everything else that exists in the universe.

SUPER SHEROES OF SCIENCE

Diana Trujillo

Stephanie Wilson

Katherine Johnson

Wang Zhenyi

The Super SHEroes of Science in this book changed the world in many different ways. They created detailed star maps, guided rockets into **orbit**, visited space as an astronaut, and are exploring Mars with a robotic rover. And many of these women started off by being told that science wasn't for them. But they stuck to their dreams, asked questions, and took risks. They eventually got to write their own stories.

This book brings their stories to you! And while you read them, remember:

Your story can change the world, too! You can become a Super SHEro of Science.

Henrietta Swan Leavitt

The universe is truly huge, but it took **astronomers** a long time to work out just how enormous it is. It was the work of Henrietta Swan Leavitt that made it possible!

SUPER SHERO OF SCIENCE

Henrietta was born into a well-off family in Massachusetts. After her family moved to Ohio, Henrietta went to a nearby college for a few years, studying music and several other subjects. Next, the Leavitts moved back to Massachusetts, where they settled near Harvard University.

datafile

Born: 1868

Died: 1921

Place of birth: United States

Field: Astronomy

Super SHEro for: Finding a way to calculate how far stars are from Earth

At the time, Harvard didn't accept women, so Henrietta joined its sister school, nicknamed the "Harvard Annex." Her favorite subjects were math and astronomy.

When Henrietta graduated in 1892, she became a volunteer at Harvard University's **observatory**. She studied photos of space, looking at the brightness of different stars. She would examine photo after photo, looking for tiny differences.

Graduates of the "Harvard Annex" in the 1890s

In 1896, Henrietta left Harvard to go traveling in Europe. She then took a teaching job in Wisconsin. She was still interested in astronomy. She wrote to her old boss at the observatory and he offered her a job back at Harvard. Henrietta became a "human computer." In those days before electronic calculators, human computers were the people who did difficult math.

Harvard observatory around the time Henrietta worked there.

Henrietta began work on variable stars. These are bright stars that fade away and then brighten up again. By comparing photos taken at different times, Henrietta could record how and when these stars changed in brightness.

What's Your Story?

?

Henrietta decided to work as an unpaid volunteer for a while so she could qualify to study astronomy.

Have you volunteered for anything?

What kind of work would you be happy to do without being paid?

Henrietta became interested in a type of variable star called a cepheid. Cepheid stars change in brightness in a regular pattern. How long one of these stars takes to grow and shrink in brightness, called its period, can be anywhere from 1 to 100 days. Henrietta identified 1,777 cepheid stars.

The Harvard human computers at work. Henrietta is sitting third from the left.

Did You Know?

In the night sky, some stars appear brighter than others. Bigger stars are usually brighter than the small ones, but the brightness of a star also depends on how far away it is from Earth. When there are two identical stars, the one that looks brightest to us is always nearer to Earth.

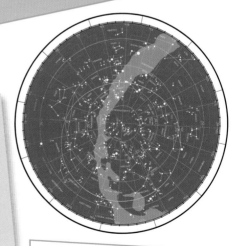

The brighter stars are shown as larger spots on star maps.

This cepheid star is 15,000 times brighter than the sun.

Henrietta then made a very important discovery. The length of a cepheid's period was linked to its size and brightness. Brighter stars had longer periods. Two variable stars with the same period were also the same size and brightness. If one of them looked dimmer than the other, then that meant the star was just farther away from us. Henrietta had discovered an easy way to measure how far away the stars were.

Henrietta's incredible breakthrough made it possible to measure the size of the universe. **Henrietta died before her discovery was put to use, but thanks to her, astronomers at last began to understand just how big—and how old—the universe really is.**

Henrietta used math to make her discovery about stars—not a telescope!

What Would You Do?

Henrietta and the other female human computers were crucial to the study of astronomy. However, the men that they worked for received the credit for their discoveries.

How would you feel if you worked on a project and were not given the same credit as your teammates?

Would it matter to you?

Katherine Johnson

SUPER
SHERO
OF SCIENCE

Flying in space is difficult. One tiny mistake could mean a spacecraft is lost forever. Katherine Johnson's amazing ability with math made sure early astronauts stayed on course and came home safely.

datafile

Born: 1918

Died: 2020

Place of birth: United States

Field: Mathematics

Super SHEro for: Calculating flight paths for astronauts

It was clear from a young age that Katherine was very clever. She was especially good with numbers. Back then, most Black girls in Virginia did not have the opportunity to go to high school. Katherine's teachers and parents spotted her amazing intelligence. She started high school at the age of ten!

Graduates of West Virginia State College.

By the time she was fourteen, Katherine joined West Virginia State College to study mathematics and French. She earned two college degrees by the age of eighteen!

Next, Katherine was handpicked to be one of the first African American students to join the graduate program at West Virginia University. She continued her studies in math but soon left to get married and start a family. After her daughters were born, Katherine became a teacher.

What's Your Story?

Katherine was singled out as a gifted student at a very young age. This gave her the chance to become a successful mathematician.

Have you ever been selected for a special talent?

Did you see it as a good opportunity?

Or would you rather have not stood out from the crowd?

Katherine working through a math problem sitting at her desk at NASA.

In 1953, Katherine took a job with the National Advisory Committee for Aeronautics (NACA). This organization worked on aircraft that could fly higher and faster than ever before. Katherine joined a group of women mathematicians called the West Area Computing Unit.

A segregated theater in the Southern United States.

The West Area Computing Unit was made up of Black women. NACA was a **segregated** organization. Katherine had to use separate bathrooms and cafeterias from the white staff.

Then in 1958, NACA changed into the National Aeronautics and Space Administration (NASA). It was set up to explore space. NASA was not segregated, so Katherine and the other Black workers started to be treated more fairly.

In 1960, Katherine worked on a project to calculate how to put a **satellite** into orbit. She was listed as one of the authors of the project report. This was the first time a woman space scientist had been recognized in this way.

Did You Know?

The first satellite was launched in 1957. It was about the size of a beachball. Today's satellites are as big as a car, and they do things like track weather systems, help with navigation, and transmit TV signals. Dozens of satellites are launched every year, but it remains a very complicated and expensive process.

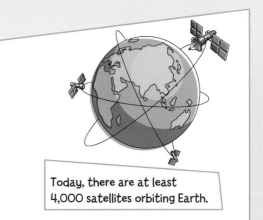

Today, there are at least 4,000 satellites orbiting Earth.

John Glenn gets ready for launch into orbit.

It was an exciting time to be working at NASA. The "Space Race" had begun, as the United States and the **Soviet Union** competed to be the first to explore space. In 1961, Katherine calculated the flight path for the spacecraft that carried Alan Shepard, the first American to travel into space.

The following year, NASA launched an astronaut into orbit for the first time. The flight path was planned by an electronic computer. The astronaut, John Glenn, did not trust the system. He asked Katherine to check all the calculations by hand. She did, and the mission was a success.

Katherine also worked on the moon landings and **space shuttle** flights. In 2015, she was awarded the Presidential Medal of Freedom. Her amazing story was told to the world in a book and a Hollywood movie called *Hidden Figures* in 2016.

Katherine used numbers and math to reach for the stars! **Thanks to her talent and hard work, she was a key part in the exploration of outer space. That adventure continues today.**

Katherine working with early computers.

What Would You Do?

Katherine wasn't an astronomer or an astronaut. She was a mathematician. But she was able to use her skills to help send explorers into space. There is math at the heart of many branches of science.

How do you think you could use math to help other people?

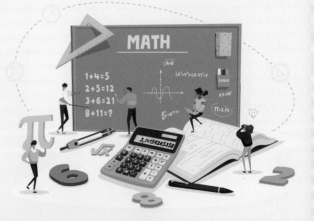

Stephanie Wilson

SUPER
SHERO
OF SCIENCE

Many children dream of flying into space one day, and Stephanie Wilson actually did it! She became a specialist astronaut and is now training to fly to the moon.

Stephanie was born in Massachusetts. As a child, she was interested in space. In junior high, Stephanie interviewed an astronomy professor from the local college. He loved his job, and Stephanie was determined to find a career that she enjoyed. Being an astronaut seemed like a good choice!

datafile

Born: 1966

Place of birth: United States

Role: Engineer and Astronaut

Super SHEro for: Spending a total of 42 days in space

Stephanie is third from the left in the front row of NASA's class of 1996.

Stephanie decided to study engineering. Thanks to training from NASA she became a rocket expert. She worked on NASA's Galileo spacecraft that was sent to explore Jupiter.

Stephanie joined NASA's astronaut program in 1996. It was only a few years earlier that Mae Jemison had become the first Black woman to travel in space. Stephanie was following in her footsteps.

What's Your Story?

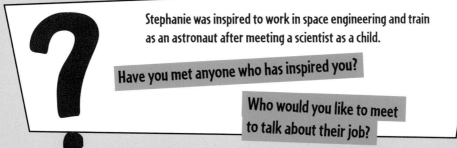

Stephanie was inspired to work in space engineering and train as an astronaut after meeting a scientist as a child.

Have you met anyone who has inspired you?

Who would you like to meet to talk about their job?

In 2010, Stephanie was one of four women in space—a record number.

Flying to space takes a lot of training. Astronauts learn how to use the systems on their spacecraft, such as the International Space Station (ISS). They learn how to move and stay healthy in the weightlessness of space.

Ten years after starting her training, Stephanie made it into space. She flew on a space shuttle. There was a fleet of shuttles, but one of them—*Columbia*—had come apart during a mission in 2003, killing the entire crew. Stephanie's mission in 2006 was only the second shuttle flight after the *Columbia* disaster.

The shuttle *Discovery* blasts off for a new mission.

She flew on the shuttle *Discovery*, delivering supplies and equipment to the ISS. Her mission also tested new safety techniques to avoid any further disasters. Stephanie's main job was operating the robotic arm that moved cargo from the shuttle to the ISS.

Stephanie operating the robotic arm on the ISS during her 2006 mission.

Did You Know?

Astronauts float around inside their spacecraft as if they are weightless! This is because they are moving along inside at exactly the same speed as the spacecraft around them. It takes some getting used to, but it looks like a lot of fun!

There is no up or down for an astronaut floating in space.

Stephanie flew on two more shuttle missions: STS-120 in 2007 and STS-131 in 2010. (All shuttle missions were numbered and start with "STS", which stands for "Space Transportation System.")

In her time with NASA, Stephanie has been part of many firsts. During STS-131, there were three women in the shuttle crew, and when they docked with the ISS, they joined Tracy Caldwell Dyson, who was already on board. This was the first time that four women were in space at the same time.

Stephanie, on the left, stands with the crew of her first space flight in 2006.

In 2019, two astronauts performed the first all-female space walk. Stephanie was on the ground at mission control, guiding them over the radio in her role as CapCom. This is the person who speaks to the crew members, and the job is always done by a fellow astronaut.

Stephanie is now one of the astronauts in NASA's Artemis Program, which will take humans back to the moon. **Stephanie's missions into space are an inspiration for tomorrow's space explorers.**

NASA is planning to send astronauts to the moon's south pole.

What Would You Do ?

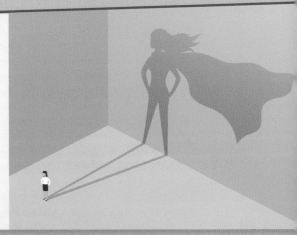

The *Columbia* disaster reminded people that space travel is dangerous. Even small malfunctions can cause big problems.

Do you think that going into space is worth the risk?

Would you have the courage it takes to do it?

At Work with Stephanie Wilson

There is no "normal" day for an astronaut like Stephanie. In space she operates robotic arms hauling loads around spacecraft. Back on the ground she helps other astronauts up in orbit.

Stephanie on board STS-131.

Before her first mission, Stephanie practices on Earth, using simulators and virtual reality (VR) systems. The space shuttle had a robotic arm. This was used for moving loads into and out of the cargo bay.

Virtual reality headset

Mission control

Stephanie at work

The ISS is fitted with an even bigger robotic arm. Stephanie is trained to operate that one as well.

The control stations for the robotic arms have several screens and keyboards, and joysticks for moving the arm. The shuttle arm could lift about 282,000 tons (256,000 metric tons)! On STS-120 and STS-131, Stephanie used the arm to add a new cabin to the space station. On STS-120, she also carried another astronaut on a space walk! He stood on the end of the arm, and Stephanie moved him around as he repaired the outside of the spacecraft.

Primary Role: Astronaut and Robotic Arm Operator

Places of work: Control stations inside the space shuttle or ISS

Daily activities: Training for future space flights, working in mission control

Main equipment: Monitors, robotic arm, joystick, radios, spacesuit, VR headset

Major collaborators: Crewmates on space station or shuttle, mission control

Robotic arm

Andrea Ghez

Not even light can escape from a **black hole**, so it's impossible to see them. But Andrea Ghez found a way to find them! She proved that a huge one is lurking at the center of our **galaxy**.

SUPER SHERO OF SCIENCE

datafile

Born: 1965

Place of birth: United States

Role: Astrophysicist

Super SHEro for: Discovering a huge black hole at the center of our galaxy, the Milky Way

When she was four years old, Andrea watched on television as Neil Armstrong took the first steps on the moon. She decided there and then to be an astronaut —at least that or a ballerina!

Andrea loved math. Numbers were like a game to her. When she went to college, she started as a math major. But she couldn't stop thinking about space and she switched to **physics**

The first moon landing in 1969 inspired many! ⬆

instead. She spent her summers working at observatories in Arizona and Chile.

Once she had her degree, Andrea attended Caltech (the California Institute of Technology) to get her PhD. She was able to work with new technology that produced clearer pictures of the stars.

What's Your Story?

Andrea taught physics classes to college students. She did this because she wanted to be a role model and encourage young women to study science.

Do you have any role models?

How do they inspire you?

Baby stars form inside swirling clouds of gas and dust called nebulas. It is very hard to see into these clouds, even with very powerful telescopes.

Andrea had become an expert at taking pictures of faint stars. She took many pictures of an area of the sky, then layered them on top of each other. This was good for getting rid of the fuzziness, but it still could not see inside the dark nebulas.

Nebulas are the nurseries where young stars form.

Next, Andrea joined a group of space scientists who were working on a way to use telescopes to pick up the heat from the hidden young stars, rather than their light.

Andrea began to study a fuzzy, dark area at the center of our galaxy. Many astronomers thought this zone had a black hole inside. But how could they find it? Black holes are invisible.

This telescope in Hawaii detects stars from their invisible heat rays.

Did You Know?

A black hole is the heaviest and smallest thing in the universe. It forms when a giant star explodes, and the leftovers are crushed smaller than a speck of dust! A black hole has an enormous pull of gravity. Nothing can escape—not even beams of light. That is why a black hole is always black.

A black hole makes a dark patch of space.

Andrea and her team picked up the heat from stars inside the dark patch. They tracked how the stars moved. They noticed some were traveling at 3 million miles per hour (5 million km/h)! That huge speed showed that the stars were being pulled on by something that weighed many, many times more than our sun.

Andrea also showed that the stars were moving around a very small object. The only thing that can be small but also heavy is a black hole.

The stars in the middle of our galaxy make a pale streak running though the night sky. This streak is also called the Milky Way.

The black hole Andrea discovered weighs 4 million times more than the sun! Her discovery is being used by other astronomers to figure out how galaxies form. Knowing that will help to explain where the universe came from! **Andrea shared the Nobel Prize in Physics for this discovery in 2020.**

Andrea shows off her Nobel Prize medal.

What Would You Do?

Andrea studies objects so far away that we can never visit. We can't even see some of them!

Would you like to study distant things you can never touch?

Or would you prefer science that has more of an impact on everyday life?

At Work with Andrea Ghez

Andrea's discovery of the Milky Way galaxy's black hole took amazing technology, a lot of teamwork–and a lot of time, too!

Andrea works mostly in an office.

Andrea works with a team of astronomers based in California. But the telescopes they use are far away! Andrea's team mainly uses the telescopes at the Keck Observatory. This is near the top of a mountain in Hawaii. It's the perfect place for looking at the stars. The night is very dark high up the mountain, and the weather is usually clear.

Telescope

Keck Observatory

Andrea at work

Places of work: Office or sometimes an observatory

Daily activities: Using math to analyze images collected by telescopes

Main equipment: Telescope, computer

Main collaborators: The Galactic Center Group at UCLA in California

Stars twinkle because our atmosphere makes the starlight "wiggle" as it travels to our eyes. The telescope that Andrea uses has a special mirror that can ripple to match the way the light wiggles. This removes the twinkling effect and gives a much clearer picture.

Andrea's team can only do their observations a few nights a year. Once she has the images, Andrea analyzes them to see what has changed since the last view. By using math, she can work out where the stars are going and how fast they are traveling.

Computer

SUPER SHEROES
OF SCIENCE

Hypatia

Born in Alexandria, Egypt, Hypatia was the daughter of a mathematician and astronomer who taught her the works of important Greek scientists. After he died, Hypatia continued his work. She gave lectures on math and astronomy. In her time, she was the world's leading mathematician.

Hypatia
(Egypt, c. 355–415 CE)

Maria Kirch

Maria Kirch
(Germany, 1670–1720)

As a girl, Maria Kirch studied astronomy and ended up marrying a fellow astronomer. They worked together in Berlin, now in Germany, to map the stars. In 1702, Maria became the first woman to discover a **comet**. She studied the *aurora borealis*, which are colored lights seen in the sky near the North Pole, and she wrote about conjunctions, which is when two planets line up in the sky.

Wang Zhenyi

Wang Zhenyi was born in China at a time when girls were not expected to go to school. But she was determined to learn and was given books by her family. She read whatever she could find—from astronomy and mathematics to poetry.

Wang Zhenyi
(China, 1768-1797)

Zhenyi loved math, and she also loved observing the stars and planets. Her knowledge of math helped her figure out why objects in the sky moved the way they did. She was especially interested in **eclipses**, and she published books and articles explaining how solar and lunar eclipses work.

More

SUPER SHEROES OF SCIENCE

Exploring **Space** STARLIGHT

Annie Jump Cannon

Annie Jump Cannon grew up in Delaware, where her mother taught her to identify constellations, or patterns of stars. An infection in childhood made Annie lose most of her hearing. She went to college to study physics and astronomy. After graduating, Annie became a human computer at the Harvard observatory, working alongside Henrietta Swan Leavitt.

Annie worked out a way of organizing stars by their colors. The colors in starlight show what each star is made of and how hot it is. Annie's system is still used today.

Annie Jump Cannon (United States, 1863-1941)

Mary Golda Ross

Mary Golda Ross
(United States, 1908-2008)

Mary Golda Ross was a member of the Cherokee Nation and grew up in eastern Oklahoma. The Cherokee value education for girls just as much as they do for boys, and Mary earned a degree in math. She worked for a while as a teacher before taking a job with the Lockheed Aircraft Corporation. The United States was fighting in World War II at the time, and Mary was part of the "Skunk Works," the company's top-secret division that designed advanced aircraft. She was the only female engineer on the team, and the only Indigenous person, as well. After the war, Mary helped to write a book about how to fly to other planets and then worked on rockets and early spacecraft designs.

Valentina Tereshkova

Valentina was an expert skydiver, and she applied to the Soviet space program in 1961. Two years later, Valentina Tereshkova made history by becoming the first woman to reach space! In 1963, she flew on the Vostok 6 mission, orbiting Earth 48 times. Valentina later became an elected politician in Russia.

Exploring **Space** PIONEER

Valentina Tereshkova
(Russia, born 1937)

Mae Jemison

American Mae Jemison trained as a medical doctor before joining NASA's astronaut program. In 1992 she became the first Black woman to fly in space, when she flew on the space shuttle *Endeavour*. Her background in medical research was put to good use. She investigated the effects of weightlessness on the human body.

Exploring **Space** SPACE MEDICINE

Mae Jemison
(United States, born 1956)

Diana Trujillo

Diana Trujillo
(Colombia, born in the early 1980s)

Diana Trujillo moved from Colombia to the United States when she was seventeen. She didn't speak English, but she took classes to learn, and she cleaned houses to pay for college. While still studying engineering in Florida, Diana got a job at NASA.

From the mission control in California, Diana operates the robotic arm on the *Perseverance* rover that is exploring Mars. The arm collects samples from the red planet's surface, looking for signs of life.

Diana hosted a live Spanish-language broadcast of *Perseverance* landing on Mars, called #JuntosPerseveramos. She gives updates on the mission, inspiring the next generation of Latinx space scientists.

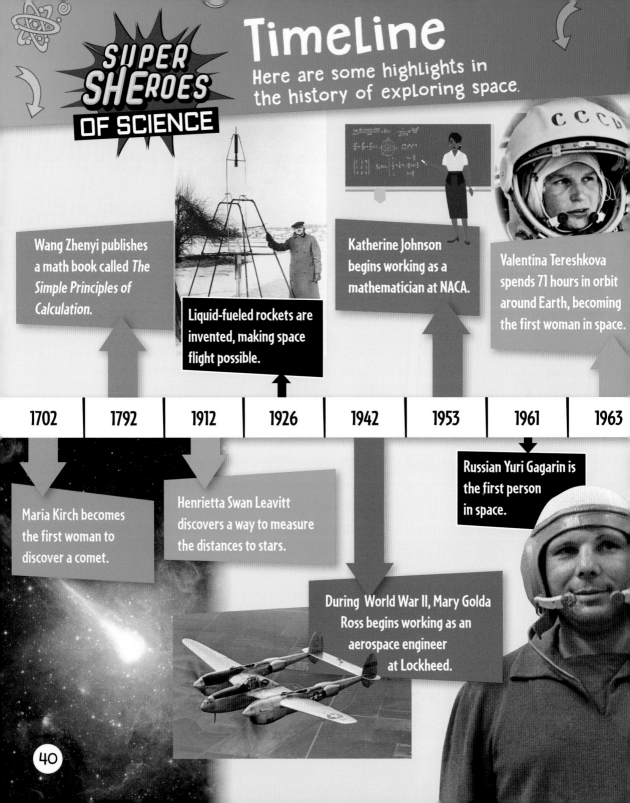

SUPER SHEROES OF SCIENCE

Timeline

Here are some highlights in the history of exploring space.

Wang Zhenyi publishes a math book called *The Simple Principles of Calculation.*

Liquid-fueled rockets are invented, making space flight possible.

Katherine Johnson begins working as a mathematician at NACA.

Valentina Tereshkova spends 71 hours in orbit around Earth, becoming the first woman in space.

| 1702 | 1792 | 1912 | 1926 | 1942 | 1953 | 1961 | 1963 |

Maria Kirch becomes the first woman to discover a comet.

Henrietta Swan Leavitt discovers a way to measure the distances to stars.

Russian Yuri Gagarin is the first person in space.

During World War II, Mary Golda Ross begins working as an aerospace engineer at Lockheed.

Diana Trujillo hosts #JuntosPerseveramos, a Spanish-language live broadcast of the *Perseverance* Mars rover landing.

The first crew arrives at the International Space Station.

President Barack Obama awards Katherine Johnson the Presidential Medal of Freedom.

| 1992 | 2000 | 2006 | 2015 | 2020 | 2021 |

Mae Jemison becomes the first Black woman to travel into space, taking part in an eight-day mission.

Stephanie Wilson takes her first voyage into space aboard the space shuttle *Discovery*.

Stephanie Wilson is chosen as an astronaut candidate for the upcoming Artemis missions to the moon.

Andrea Ghez wins the Nobel Prize in Physics for her part in the discovery of a supermassive black hole at the center of the Milky Way galaxy .

SUPER SHEROES OF SCIENCE

Where in the World?

1. Annie Jump Cannon
Cambridge, Massachusetts
Annie worked at the observatory at Harvard University, setting up a way to organize stars by their colors.

2. Andrea Ghez
Los Angeles, California
Andrea lived in New York and Chicago and is now a professor at UCLA in California, where she investigates the center of our galaxy.

3. Hypatia
Alexandria, Egypt
Hypatia lived and worked in Alexandria at a time when the ancient Greeks ruled Egypt.

4. Mae Jemison
Chicago, Illinois
Mae grew up in Chicago, but her work as a doctor, astronaut, and business leader has taken her all over the world.

5. Katherine Johnson
Hampton, Virginia
Katherine worked as a human computer at a NASA laboratory in Virginia. A building on the site is now named for her.

6. Maria Kirch
Berlin, Germany
Mary and her husband lived and worked in Berlin, where they surveyed the stars.

7. Henrietta Swan Leavitt
Cambridge, Massachusetts
Henrietta spent most of her career working at the observatory that was part of Harvard University.

8. Mary Golda Ross
Tahlequah, Oklahoma
Mary went to school in Tahlequah, the capital of the Cherokee Nation, and later worked as an aerospace engineer for Lockheed in California.

10. Diana Trujillo
Cali, Colombia
Diana was born and raised in Colombia before moving to the United States to study and eventually work for NASA.

11. Stephanie Wilson
Houston, Texas
Stephanie grew up in Massachusetts, worked as a rocket engineer in California, and then did her NASA astronaut training at Johnson Space Center in Texas.

12. Wang Zhenyi
Nanjing, China
Zhenyi grew up in China, where her parents and grandparents encouraged her love of learning.

9. Valentina Tereshkova
Baikonur, Kazakhstan
Valentina lifted off from the Baikonur Cosmodrome in what is now Kazakhstan. At the time this was part of the Soviet Union.

Arctic Ocean

Europe

6.

3.

9.

Asia

Pacific Ocean

Africa

12.

Indian Ocean

Australia

Southern Ocean

Words of Wisdom

Read the inspirational words of these
Super SHEroes of Science and remember:
You can become a Super SHEro, too!

Stephanie Wilson

66 I think that there is a great thirst for knowledge, and humans have always wanted to explore. 99

Katherine Johnson

66 Like what you do, and then you will do your best. I like to learn. That's an art and a science. 99

66 I was brought up in the Cherokee tradition of equal education for boys and girls. It did not bother me to be the only girl in the math class. 99

Mary Golda Ross

66 Never be limited by other people's limited imaginations. 99

Mae Jemison

44

66 If you are determined to do what you want to do in your life, you will find a way. **99**

Diana Trujillo

Andrea Ghez

66 In high school I started to become aware of the fact that perhaps not the entire world thought that girls should be doing math, and I took this on as a challenge. **99**

66 There were times that I had to put down my pen and sigh. But I love the subject, I do not give up. **99**

Wang Zehnyi

66 If women can be railroad workers in Russia, why can't they fly in space? **99**

Valentina Tereshkova

45

Glossary

astronomer (uh-**strah**-nuh-mer) a scientist who studies space and the objects in it

black hole (**blak**-hole) object in space with gravity so strong that light and matter cannot escape it

comet (**kah**-mit) icy object in space that travels in a long, looping path around the sun, forming a long, bright tail as it melts

eclipse (i-**klips**) when the sun or moon is blocked from view because of another object traveling between it and Earth

engineer (*en*-juh-**neer**) a person who designs, builds, or maintains engines, machines, or structures

galaxy (**gal**-uhk-see) group of billions of stars and other objects that is held together by gravity. There are many billions of galaxies in the universe.

gravity (**grav**-i-tee) the force that attracts an object toward another

Milky Way (**mil**-kee way) the galaxy that includes the Earth and our solar system

Nobel Prize (no-**bell** pryz) a prize awarded for achievements in science, writing, and peacemaking

observatory (uhb-**zur**-vuh-*tor*-ee) building designed for studying space. Most observatories house telescopes.

orbit (**or**-bit) the roughly circular path that an object takes around a planet, moon, or other object

physics (**fiz**-iks) the science of matter and energy, and of their relationship

satellite (**sat**-uh-*lite*) an uncrewed spacecraft that orbits Earth

segregated (**seg**-ri-*gated*) organized so that people of different races have to stay separate

simulator (**sim**-yuh-*lay*-tur) a machine that is a realistic imitation of a real system, used for training

Soviet Union (**soh**-vee-et **yoon**-yuhn) the name for a former country made up of Russia and several smaller surrounding states

space shuttle (**spays shuht**-uhl) an old type of reusable NASA spacecraft designed to carry astronauts into space and back

Index

Page numbers in **bold** refer to illustrations

Further Reading

Dickmann, Nancy. *Women Scientists in Astronomy and Space*. Milwaukee, WI: Gareth Stevens, 2018.

Ignotofsky, Rachel. *Women in Science: 50 Fearless Pioneers Who Changed the World*. New York: Ten Speed Press, 2016.

Jackson, Tom. *What's Inside a Black Hole?* Milwaukee, WI: Gareth Stevens, 2018.

Jina, Devika. *The Extraordinary Life of Katherine Johnson*. New York: Puffin, 2019.

Ottaviani, Jim. *Astronauts: Women on the Final Frontier*. New York: First Second, 2020.

About the Author

Nancy Dickmann grew up reading encyclopedias for fun, and after many years working in children's publishing, she now has her dream job as a full-time author. She has had over 200 titles published so far, mainly on science topics, and finds that the best part of the job is researching and learning new things. One highlight was getting to interview a real astronaut to find out about using the toilet in space!

About the Consultant

Isabel Thomas is a science communicator and American Association for the Advancement of Science award-winning author. She has degrees in Human Sciences from the University of Oxford and in Education Research from the University of Cambridge, where her academic research focused on addressing inequalities in aspiration and access to science education and careers.